Thematic Units...

from The MAILBOX® magazine.

An Out-Of-This-World Adventure!

Exploring The Solar System

If you're planning a study of the solar system, be sure to consider these supplemental literature-based activities before preparing your youngsters for blastoff.

ideas contributed by Wendy Waterman

Postcards From Outer Space

Take a unique trip through the solar system with the help of a one-of-a-kind book entitled *Postcards From The Planets.* This story unfolds as Jessie and Kate depart into space in the year 2095. The twosome chronicle their experiences by writing and sending postcards to their relatives living on Earth. While the book's story line is fictional, the information about the planets has been thoroughly researched. (Available as a Big Book or in packets of six small books each, *Postcards From The Planets* may be purchased from RIGBY publishers by calling 1-800-822-8661.)

After each postcard has been read and discussed, ask your students to choose the solar system locations they would most like to visit. Pair the youngsters according to their preferences; then challenge each twosome to research its destination. To complete the project, have each pair create and complete a postcard like the ones featured in the book. Display the completed projects on a bulletin board entitled "Postcards From Outer Space!"

More About The Solar System

The Planets In Our Solar System by Franklyn M. Branley (published by Thomas Y. Crowell Junior Books) introduces the solar system and its nine planets. The author's simple text enables young readers and listeners to grasp basic facts about the solar system's celestial bodies. In addition directions for making two models of the solar system are given. One model shows the differences in the sizes of the planets. The second model can be displayed on a wall and shows the nine planets and their distances from the Sun. Another highly informative book about the solar system is *A Book About Planets And Stars* by Betty Polisar Reigot (published by Scholastic Inc.). Packed with information, this is another book worth considering for your solar system library.

Solar System Extravaganza

Showcase an eye-catching reproduction of the solar system on your playground using string, nine tubes (from paper products), and tagboard cutouts to represent the Sun and each of the nine planets. Label a tube for each planet. Cut string lengths using the chart below and wrap each length of string around the appropriate tube. Use a hole puncher to punch a hole in the left side of each planet cutout. Punch either one large hole or nine small holes in the right side of the Sun cutout. Assign each of nine student groups a planet; then distribute the tubes and planet cutouts to the appropriate groups. On the playground, position the Sun cutout in an open area. Seat the students (in their groups) near the Sun cutout. Then, in turn, have each group attach one end of its string to the Sun cutout and walk away from the Sun, gently rolling out the string on its tube. When the string's end is reached, the corresponding planet is attached. Continue in this fashion until all of the planets are displayed. Wow! What a solar system!

Planet	Distance From The Sun	String Length
Mercury	36 million miles	1 yard
Venus	67 million miles	approx. 2 yards
Earth	93 million miles	approx. 2.5 yards
Mars	142 million miles	approx. 4 yards
Jupiter	484 million miles	approx. 13.5 yards
Saturn	885 million miles	approx. 24.5 yards
Uranus	1,780 million miles	approx. 49.5 yards
Neptune	2,790 million miles	approx. 77.5 yards
Pluto	3,660 million miles	approx. 101.5 yards

Jackson Crane

Shooting Stars

The topic of shooting stars—those streaks of light that have long fascinated sky watchers—is sure to evoke an enthusiastic response from your youngsters. Ask students to share their knowledge and questions about shooting stars. Next challenge students to listen carefully as you read aloud *Shooting Stars* by Franklyn M. Branley (published by Thomas Y. Crowell Junior Books). Delightfully illustrated, this informative book explains what shooting stars are, what they are made of, and what happens when they land on Earth. At the conclusion of the book, the author states that some people believe that a wish made upon a shooting star is a wish that will come true.

After reviewing the contents of the book, create this unique class booklet of shooting-star wishes. To make a booklet page, fold a sheet of 9" x 12" construction paper in half and glue the outer edges to form a pocket. Draw and color a night sky scene on the front of the pocket and personalize the back of the pocket. Then, on a slip of paper, write and personalize your wish for a shooting star. Fold the programmed slip in half and tuck it inside the pocket. Bind the pockets between a construction-paper cover labeled "Shooting-Star Wishes." Place the completed project in your classroom library for all to enjoy.

What Is A Black Hole In Space?

Why does lightning continuously flash on Jupiter? Why is Venus's atmosphere so hard to see through? Why do stars twinkle? All of these questions and many more can be answered using the hands-on experiments in Janice VanCleave's *Astronomy For Every Kid: 101 Easy Experiments That Really Work* (published by John Wiley & Sons, Inc.). Written especially for young children, each experiment is presented with its purpose, a list of needed materials, step-by-step instructions, expected results, and a scientific explanation in terms that kids can understand. In fact, each experiment has been "child tested" by the author's own students. Using the experiments in this valuable resource, you can propel your students' science enthusiasm to extraordinary heights!

Out-Of-This-World Poetry

Send your youngsters into orbit with this poetry-writing activity. For an inspiring introduction to space-related poetry, read aloud selected poems from *Space Songs* by poet Myra Cohn Livingston (published by Holiday House, Inc.). Display a length of colorful bulletin-board paper. Write the name of a planet at the top of the paper, and enlist from your youngsters words and phrases that describe the planet. Write each description on the paper, arranging the words in a desired fashion. When the poem is complete, ask students to join in as you read it aloud. Next divide students into small groups and give each group a length of colorful bulletin-board paper and a marker. Working as a team, have each group agree upon a space-related topic and create a poem about it. After each group has shared its poem, post the completed projects in a school hallway for others to enjoy.

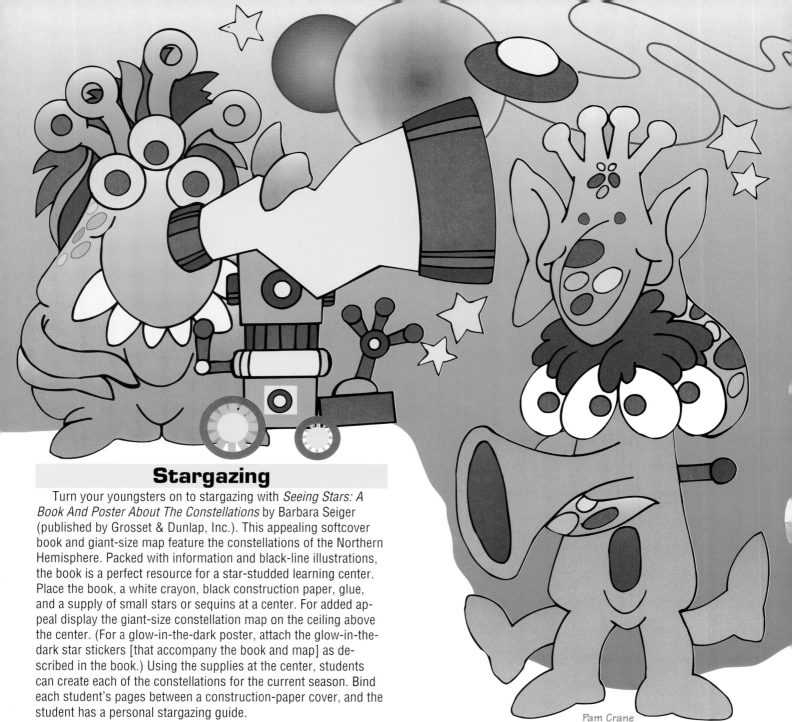

Stargazing

Turn your youngsters on to stargazing with *Seeing Stars: A Book And Poster About The Constellations* by Barbara Seiger (published by Grosset & Dunlap, Inc.). This appealing softcover book and giant-size map feature the constellations of the Northern Hemisphere. Packed with information and black-line illustrations, the book is a perfect resource for a star-studded learning center. Place the book, a white crayon, black construction paper, glue, and a supply of small stars or sequins at a center. For added appeal display the giant-size constellation map on the ceiling above the center. (For a glow-in-the-dark poster, attach the glow-in-the-dark star stickers [that accompany the book and map] as described in the book.) Using the supplies at the center, students can create each of the constellations for the current season. Bind each student's pages between a construction-paper cover, and the student has a personal stargazing guide.

Pam Crane

Life On Other Planets

Most youngsters (and adults!) are intrigued by the thought of extraterrestrial neighbors. In Franklyn M. Branley's book *Is There Life In Outer Space?* (published by Thomas Y. Crowell Junior Books), the author discusses several ideas and misconceptions about life in outer space. After reading the book aloud, ask youngsters to recap why most scientists do not believe there is life on the other planets in our solar system. Take a class poll to determine how many students believe that there could be other planets beyond our solar system. Also find out if they think other forms of life may or may not be living on these planets. (See "Alien Artwork" for a far-out follow-up activity!)

Alien Artwork

Send your youngsters into orbit with this totally cosmic project! To set the mood, read aloud a book that features an alien character such as *UFO Diary* by Satoshi Kitamura (published by Farrar Straus Giroux), *Earthlets As Explained By Professor Xargle* by Jeanne Willis (published by E. P. Dutton), or *Space Case* by Edward Marshall (published by Dial Books For Young Readers). Invite each student to imagine the perfect alien and illustrate it on a large sheet of drawing paper. Then have each youngster answer questions about his alien friend by completing a copy of page 7. Be sure to provide time for students to introduce their alien friends to their classmates. Far-out!

Introducing An Alien

Answer each question about the alien you illustrated.
Use complete sentences.

1. What is this alien's name? _____

_____

2. Where is this alien from? _____

_____

3. How old is this alien? _____

_____

4. What was this alien's life like before it came to Earth? _____

_____

_____

5. What does this alien like to eat? _____

_____

6. What does this alien like to do for fun? _____

_____

7. What is one thing you hope to learn from your alien friend? _____

_____

8. What is one thing you hope to teach your alien friend? _____

_____

Note To Teacher: Use this activity with "Alien Artwork" on page 6.

News Travels Fast!

_____

soared to
extraordinary heights

_____

_____

_____

Congratulations!

©The Education Center, Inc.

_____

was observed

_____

_____

Thank you for your thoughtfulness!

©The Education Center, Inc.

Mission Accomplished!

_____

earned this award

_____

_____

_____

Hooray For You!

©The Education Center, Inc.

Far Out,

_____!

Your

_____

_____

_____

was
out-of-this-world!

©The Education Center, Inc.

By The Light Of The Silvery Moon

Begin to unravel the seemingly mystical qualities of the Moon with this collection of multidisciplinary ideas and reproducibles.

ideas contributed by Karen Shelton

Moon Magic

What can grow larger or smaller, disappear, and reappear right before our eyes? That's right—the Moon! But the Moon itself does not really change. As it travels around the earth, half of the Moon is always lighted by the Sun. The Moon phases occur because, from the earth, we do not always see the entire lit portion of the Moon.

To demonstrate the various Moon phases, make a Moon viewer. Cover the inside of a shoe box with black paper. Using an X-acto® knife, cut a circle (into which a flashlight can be snugly inserted) and eight square openings from the sides and ends of the shoe box. Cover the outer surface of each square opening by taping a black construction-paper flap atop it. Duplicate, cut out, and mount the labels on page 12 on the viewer as shown on that page. Suspend a golf ball from the center of the shoe box lid using a rubber band. Place the lid on the box. Insert a flashlight into the circular opening. To use the Moon viewer, turn on the flashlight (the Sun). One at a time, raise each paper flap and view the suspended ball (the Moon) in its labeled phase.

Bill O'Connor

More About Moon Magic!

The Moon Seems To Change by Franklyn M. Branley (A Let's-Read-and-Find-Out Book) is an excellent resource for further explanation of the Moon's phases. In addition to the colorful diagrams and easy-to-read text, the book includes a simple Moon phase experiment requiring only an orange, a pencil, and a flashlight. It's a must for your Moon explorers!

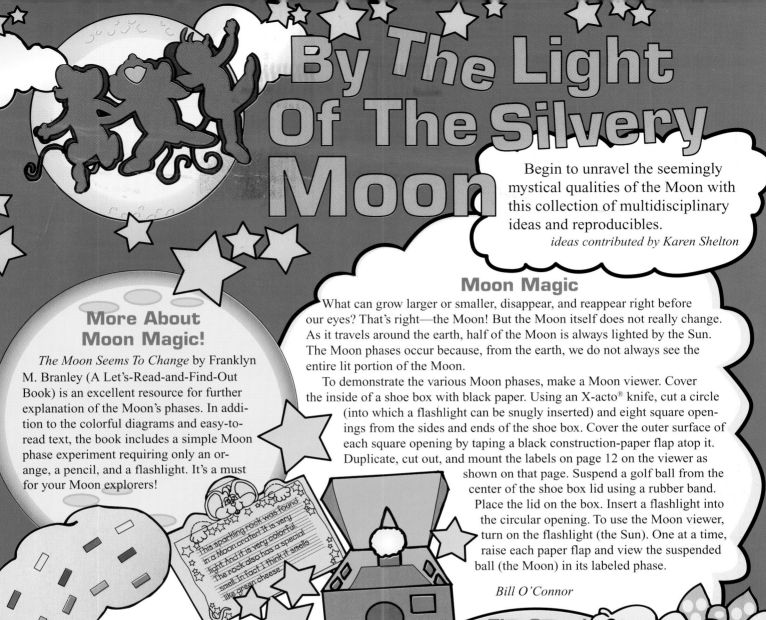

This sparkling rock was found in a Moon crater! It is very light. And it is very colorful. The rock also has a special smell. In fact I think it smells like green cheese.

Moon Rocks

If the man in the Moon goes for a stroll, he's likely to stir up a lot of gray dust, tiny colored glass balls, and Moon rocks—but no green cheese. Encourage your youngsters to make "Moon rocks" and then combine their projects to create a Moon rock museum exhibit. For every five students, mix together 2 cups flour, 1 cup salt, clear or silver glitter, a small amount of black tempera paint, and enough water to achieve a play dough consistency. Have each student shape a portion of dough into a Moon rock, before pressing tiny colored beads into its surface. Allow the projects to harden. Display each Moon rock with a student-written description. Then invite neighboring classes to visit your Moon rock exhibit. If desired, duplicate student copies of page 13 onto construction paper. Have students write rock descriptions on the lines and complete the discovery information, then cut on the dotted lines and fold to create display tags as shown. Smithsonian, beware—this Moon rock exhibit will be a hit!

The Sound Of Silence

Moonbeams shed their silvery light on the quieter part of most people's day. This seems fitting since there is absolutely no sound on the Moon. Sound travels through air. But since the Moon has no air, sounds can't be transmitted without communication devices. Have your students sit silently and listen to the sounds around them. Find out what quiet places they have visited. If they were on the Moon, how would your youngsters like the total quiet?

Have students pretend they are Moon visitors whose communication devices have temporarily stopped working. Taking turns, have students silently act out words and phrases for the remainder of the class. Use these words to begin with: Big Dipper, man in the Moon, lift-off, shuttle, blue Moon, crater, Milky Way, Moon rock.

LEVI'S

Telephone Call

lightbulb

Exploring New Worlds

Imagine how Columbus and his crew must have felt as they launched their ships through uncharted waters toward an unexplored land. Before the *Niña, Pinta,* and the *Santa María* reached the New World, more than two months had elapsed. Even though a trek to the Moon is 60 times farther than Columbus' voyage to the New World, we can now travel 1,000 times faster than Columbus did. A trip to the Moon takes only three days by spaceship!

In the 500 years since Columbus arrived in the New World, technological advances have been tremendous. To illustrate this, mount and label five sentence strips on an empty, horizontal wall space. Read aloud Jean Fritz's *Where Do You Think You're Going, Christopher Columbus?* to give students a feel for the lack of technology during Columbus' lifetime. Ask one child to draw Columbus or his ship on a construction paper mouse cutout (pattern on page 12), label it, and mount it below the timeline. Then, as you discuss each of the scientific and industrial advances in the list, have a student add an appropriate symbol to your timeline.

Clock

1492—Columbus "discovers" the New World.
1631—First ship built in the colonies is launched.
1752—Benjamin Franklin, flying his kite in a storm, makes discoveries about electricity.
1754—First American-made clock is built.
1787—Steam-powered, paddle-propelled boat gets a trial run.
1850—Levi Strauss makes canvas pants, called Levi's®, for gold miners.
1876—Alexander Graham Bell makes the first understandable telephone call.
1877—Thomas Edison makes the first recording using a phonograph.
1879—Edison invents the first practical, electric lightbulb.
1903—Orville Wright takes the first sustained, controlled, powered flight on a heavier-than-air machine.
1903—Henry Ford's new automobile company makes one Model T Ford every hour.
1924—Television system is patented.
1926—First liquid-fuel rocket is launched.
1944—First major digital computer operates at Harvard.
1961—Alan Shepard makes the first American spaceflight.
1969—Neil Armstrong walks on the Moon.
1981—First reusable manned spacecraft, the shuttle *Columbia,* is launched into space.

Breathtaking Lunar Landmarks

It's often with wistful "if only" sighs that people gaze at the Moon above. Have your students imagine themselves as futuristic travel agents who entice earthlings to visit the Moon. Have each student illustrate and compose an enticing written description of one or all of the lunar sights or landmarks listed below. Encourage students to present their information in a "travel brochure" or poster format. To get students started, first show them some literature obtained from a travel agent. Point out the colorful and descriptive language that is used to persuade readers.

Stars—From the Moon, you can see many more stars than can be seen from Earth. Because the Moon has no atmosphere, stars appear 20 times brighter than on Earth and their lights do not appear to flicker.
Earth—In the Moon's sky, Earth is a blue ball four times larger than the Moon appears to be from Earth. From the Moon, Earth goes through phases exactly like the Moon does when viewed from Earth.
Tranquility Base—This location is the historic landing place of Neil Armstrong and Buzz Aldrin, the first men on the Moon. Their TV camera (with tripod), two backpacks, some overshoes, a nylon American flag, and the astronauts' footprints can be viewed here.
Copernicus Crater—This crater has a ten-mile mountain range in its bed, surrounded by a rim that juts up two to three miles.
Straight Wall—This steep cliff, about 80 miles in length and two miles high, casts an eerie shadow. Step into the shadow and you will appear to have completely disappeared. This is because without air, dust particles are not present to carry light into the shadow.

New Worlds On The Horizon

Having completed a 500-year timeline, it may be apparent to your youngsters that we've explored many new worlds since Columbus' time and that visiting other heavenly bodies, such as the Moon, is a relatively new undertaking. Ask your youngsters to predict how man will interact with the Moon and other "new worlds" within the next 500 years. Hint: It has been predicted that the Moon will serve as the location for a populated U.S. space communication base and that minerals may be extracted from lunar soils.

Lunar Lingo

Our language is littered with Moon-related words. *Month,* for example, comes from the Old English word for Moon. Because early civilizations realized that the phases of the Moon progressed in four-week cycles, this period of time came to be known as a *moonth.* Eventually moonth became *month.* Since the first month of marriage is often believed to be the sweetest, a married couple's first month together came to be called a *honeymoon.* Today, a honeymoon is usually associated with a trip or vacation a newly married couple takes—even though it may last just a few days rather than a month. The word *Monday* comes from the Anglo-Saxon word *mōnandaeg,* meaning "Moon's day." It was so named because, in ancient times, the second day of the week was dedicated to the goddess of the Moon.

Send student pairs to the library to uncover multiple meanings and the Moon-related significance of the words listed. Have each pair explain the meaning of their word in a jingle, song, or rap performed before their classmates.

moonlight	moonbeam	Moon buggy
Moon	mooncalf	moonlet
moonlit	moonquake	moonscape
lunatic	lunar	harvest moon
man in the Moon	honeymoon	moonshine
moonless	moonstruck	blue moon

One Of Many Moons

Our Moon is only one of at least 60 in our solar system. Have each of your students create a unique, paper, Moon cutout and then use it as a springboard to creative thinking. To make a paper Moon, mix 1/2 cup each of liquid soap, white tempera paint, and water in a pie pan. Then, using a straw, blow into the mixture until the bubbles rise well above the rim of the pie pan. After choosing a colorful construction-paper sheet, press it slowly onto the bubble surface until the paper is resting on the pie-pan rim. Remove the paper and allow to dry. Cut into a circular or crescent shape. Have students display and describe the physical characteristics of the Moons they have created.

Moon Jumping

Amaze students with the fact that on the Moon they could jump about six times higher than they can jump on Earth! Explain that, because the pull of gravity is less on the Moon, a person can exert the same amount of effort and jump much higher. Vertically mount a length of bulletin board paper, placing the lower edge of the paper against the floor. Measure and indicate each six-inch distance (from the floor) on the paper.

Duplicate and distribute student copies of page 14. Divide students into groups of five or less. In turn, seat the groups facing the display. One at a time, have each member stand before his group and jump as high as he can from a standing position. Between yourself and the seated members, agree upon the measurement of the jump; then have all members record the measurement on their papers. Use calculators to convert the earth jumps to approximate "Moon jumps." Then have each student complete his chart by choosing amazing feats that could be accomplished if each "Moon jump" were made on Earth!

30 in.

24 in.

18 in.

12 in.

6 in.

Frolicking Under A Full Moon

Add some fun and fantasy to your Moon activities by reading aloud *Barn Dance!* by Bill Martin Jr. and John Archambault. This toe-tappin' tale, set under the light of a full moon, is the perfect reading choice for your Moon unit.

Patterns

Use labels with "Moon Magic" on page 9.

New Moon	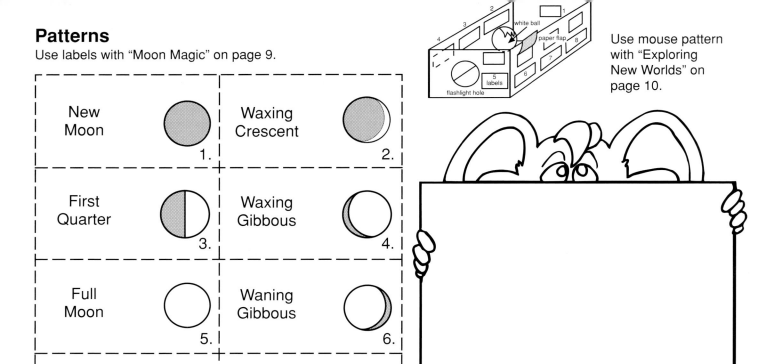 1.	Waxing Crescent	2.
First Quarter	3.	Waxing Gibbous	4.
Full Moon	5.	Waning Gibbous	6.
Last Quarter	7.	Waning Crescent	8.

Use mouse pattern with "Exploring New Worlds" on page 10.

white ball
paper flap
labels
flashlight hole

©The Education Center, Inc.

Award

Present copies of this award to students upon completion of the Moon unit.

©The Education Center, Inc. • *Solar System* • Primary • TEC3194

BIG CHEESE!

Big Cheese Award

has earned the

for
learning about the Moon!

_____
student

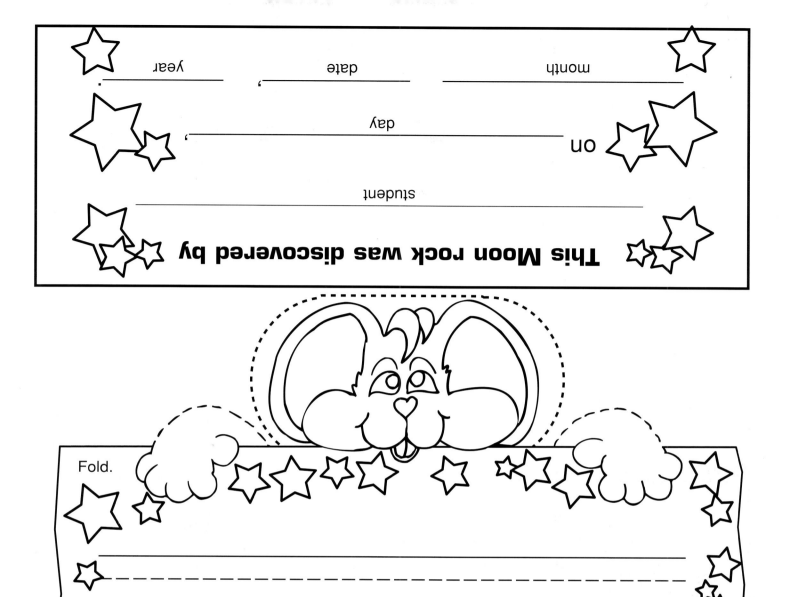

This Moon rock was discovered by

student

on

day

month , date , year .

Fold.

©The Education Center, Inc. • *Solar System* • Primary • TEC3194

Measurement and calculator activity

Moon Jumping

Fill in the chart.

Student Name	Earth Jump	Approximate Conversion	Moon Jump	An Amazing Feat
Milo Mouse	6 inches	x 6 =	36 inches or 3 feet	Milo could jump onto a picnic table.
	inches	x 6 =		
	inches	x 6 =		
	inches	x 6 =		
	inches	x 6 =		
	inches	x 6 =		

Choose from these items or measure to find your own amazing feat!

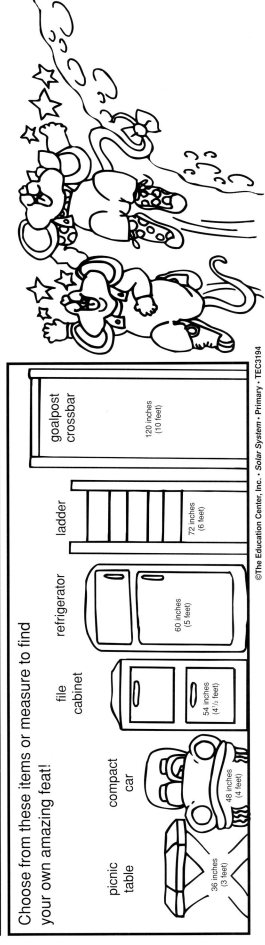

picnic table — 36 inches (3 feet)

compact car — 48 inches (4 feet)

file cabinet — 54 inches (4½ feet)

refrigerator — 60 inches (5 feet)

ladder — 72 inches (6 feet)

goalpost crossbar — 120 inches (10 feet)

Note To Teacher: See "Moon Jumping" on page 11.

14

A Pocketful Of Science

Moon Talk

Use these hands-on activities to introduce facts about the Moon.

ideas by Ann Flagg

Activity 1: Sizing Up The Moon

For each student, you will need:
one small index card   scissors

What to do:

Ask students to close their eyes and imagine the Moon and a star in their minds. While the youngsters' eyes are closed, have a show of hands to find out how many students "see" the Moon as the larger of the two objects. Then ask students to open their eyes. Explain that the following activity will help them understand why the Moon looks larger than the stars in the sky when, in fact, the Moon is much smaller than the stars we see.

To begin, have each child fold his index card in half; then starting at the fold, have him cut a large rectangle from the center of the folded card. Next have students unfold their cards and carry the resulting *frames* outside onto the playground. As a safety measure, pair students and designate a *scientist* and a *spotter* in each pair. Have each scientist close one eye and use his open eye to look at the playground area through his frame. Ask the scientists to zero in on a playground object. (The entire object must be seen through the frame.) Then have the scientists move slowly toward the objects. (Instruct the spotters to warn the scientists of obstacles in their path and to prevent collisions between students.) Periodically ask the scientists to stop and explain what is happening to the objects they're viewing. When a scientist reaches his object, he and his partner switch roles and repeat the activity. Return to the classroom when all students have participated as scientists and spotters.

Questions to ask:
1. What happened to the object inside your frame as you walked toward it?
2. Why do you think the object seemed to grow as you approached it?
3. How does this activity help you understand why the Moon looks larger than the stars, when it really isn't?

This is why:

Children often consider the Moon to be larger than the stars they see and about the same size as the Sun. The Moon has this appearance because it is Earth's closest neighbor. If the Moon and the Sun were placed side by side, the Moon would be about 400 times smaller than the Sun, which is a medium-sized star!

Activity 2: On The Move

You will need:
a handheld poster labeled for each of the following:
    "Earth," "Moon," "Sun"
an open area such as the school gym or playground

What to do:

Gather students in the open area. Select one child to hold the "Sun" sign. As you position the Sun in the center of the open area, facing her classmates, explain that *the Sun is the center of our solar system*. Select another child to hold the "Earth" sign. As you position the earth about two yards away from the Sun, explain that *Earth revolves (or moves) around the Sun*. Then set Earth in motion by asking her to maintain her distance from the Sun as she slowly walks around it. Choose another child to hold the "Moon" sign. Explain that *the Moon revolves around the earth*. Then help the Moon slide into place and begin walking around the earth as the earth revolves around the Sun. As soon as Earth has completed one revolution around the Sun, enlist three different children to re-create the solar scenario. If time permits, allow each youngster a chance to participate in the reenactment.

Once students understand the relationships between these three celestial bodies, explain that both the earth and the Moon spin like tops as they revolve around the Sun. The Sun also spins and is constantly revolving around the center of the Milky Way galaxy. Older students may wish to incorporate these spins into their demonstrations.

Questions to ask:
1. Why do you think the Sun is called the center of our solar system?
2. How is the Moon's orbit different from Earth's?

This is why:

The Sun is considered the center of our solar system because Earth and the other eight planets in our solar system travel around it. Earth travels around the Sun approximately once every 365 1/4 days. The Moon travels around Earth approximately once every 29 1/2 days with reference to the Sun, making the Moon's orbit much shorter than Earth's.

Follow-up:

Give each student two brads and a construction-paper copy of page 17. Then, following the directions on the page, have each student color and cut out the Sun, Moon, and Earth pieces and assemble the project as described. Provide assistance as needed.

Pam Crane

Activity 3: Misunderstood Moonlight

You will need:

sunlight   a hand mirror   a powerful flashlight

What to do:

While your students are out of the classroom, set up a mirror so that it catches the Sun and reflects a bright spot of light onto a conspicuous classroom location. When the students return and notice the reflection, ask them what could be causing the bright spot of light. After a bit of discussion, direct their attention to the mirror. Find out how many students think the mirror is the source of the light. Next move the mirror out of the Sun's path and turn off the lights in the room. After the students have noted that the mirror makes no light, shine the flashlight onto the mirror. Guide students to conclude that the mirror makes no light of its own; however light can bounce off (or *reflect* from) the mirror, causing it to shine.

Questions to ask:

1. In this demonstration, what do you think represents the Moon?
2. If the Moon has no light of its own, why does it appear to shine and glow at night?
3. What do you think shines on the Moon?

This is why:

Like the mirror, the Moon makes no light of its own—it is not a luminous body. The Moon shines by reflecting sunlight. Like Earth, half of the Moon is always lighted by the Sun's direct rays, and the other half is always in shadow. The Moon has phases because as the Moon travels around Earth, different parts of its bright side are seen from Earth. Without the Sun, there would be no moonlight.

Activity 4: Countless Craters

In advance:

(For the best results, plan this activity around the time of a full moon.)

To begin, ask each youngster to draw and color a full moon from memory on a sheet of drawing paper. After each student has personalized his work and labeled it "Memory Moon," collect the drawings. Next have each child personalize a second sheet of paper and label it "Moon Observation." Have students take these papers home. Ask students to observe the Moon that evening, draw and color exactly what they see on their papers, and return the illustrations to school the following school day.

For each student, you will need:

a widemouthed plastic cup half-filled with flour, cornstarch, or baking soda   one marble   "Memory Moon" drawing   "Moon Observation" drawing

What to do:

Ask students to compare and contrast their two Moon drawings. Most likely a few of the observation drawings will include gray patches or black spots on the Moon's surface. Direct students' attention to these patches and ask them to speculate what they might be. After some discussion, explain that the Moon's surface contains broad flat plains, rough mountainous highlands, and billions of craters (the most numerous feature). When viewed with an unaided eye, these features appear as dark patches. Further explain that the craters are formed when solid objects hurl through space and crash into the Moon.

To demonstrate how craters are formed, disburse the cup and marble supplies listed above. Have each student tap his cup atop his desk to level its contents, then hold his marble over the cup so that the marble is even with the cup rim. On your signal, have all students release the marbles into their cups. Ask students to examine the resulting craters; then have each student carefully remove his marble and level the contents of his cup before repeating the procedure—this time dropping the marble into the cup from several inches above the cup rim.

Questions to ask:

1. How did the size of the first crater compare to the size of the second crater? Why?
2. Do you think a heavier marble would make a bigger crater? Why or why not?

This is why:

The solar system is filled with solid objects—meteoroids—that travel through space. Unlike Earth, the Moon does not have a protective shield or atmosphere that helps to slow down, melt, or break apart these hurling objects. Most of the small craters on the Moon were formed by the impacts of meteoroids crashing into the Moon's surface. The larger craters were probably formed by larger celestial bodies (like asteroids and comets) hitting the Moon's surface. The largest crater on the Moon—the Imbrium Basin—is 700 miles wide!

Literature Connection

Noted astronomer Dr. E. C. Krupp introduces young readers to our nearest celestial neighbor in *The Moon And You* (published by Macmillan Publishing Company). This outstanding resource book includes fascinating, up-to-date information on gravity, tides, the Moon's phases, and Moon mythology.

Out-Of-This-World Orbits!

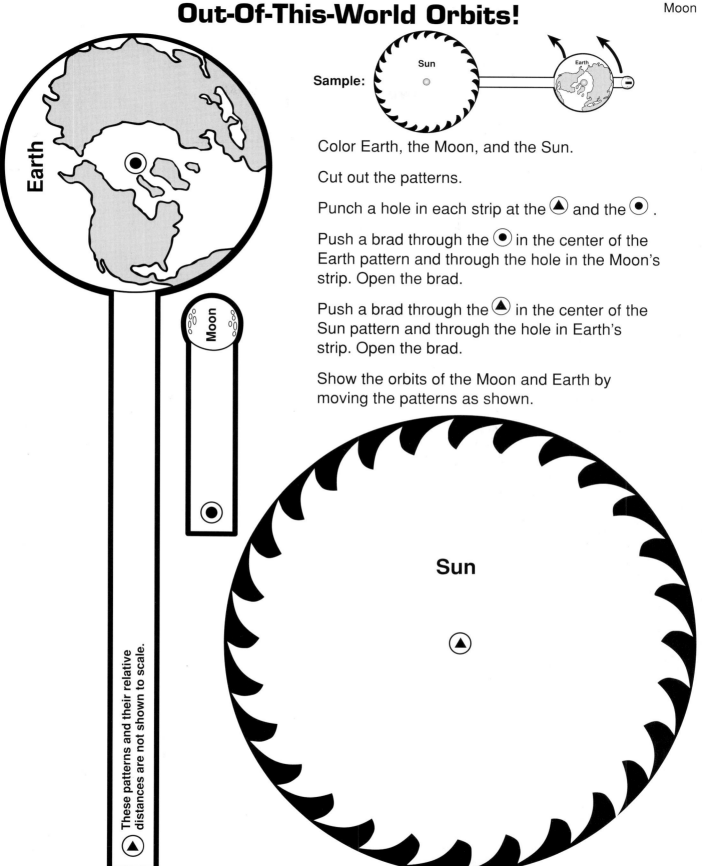

Sample:

Color Earth, the Moon, and the Sun.

Cut out the patterns.

Punch a hole in each strip at the ▲ and the ⊙ .

Push a brad through the ⊙ in the center of the Earth pattern and through the hole in the Moon's strip. Open the brad.

Push a brad through the ▲ in the center of the Sun pattern and through the hole in Earth's strip. Open the brad.

Show the orbits of the Moon and Earth by moving the patterns as shown.

These patterns and their relative distances are not shown to scale.

Note To Teacher: Use this activity after completing "Activity 2: On The Move" on page 15. Each student needs two brads, crayons, and scissors, and access to a hole puncher.

17

Moon Cookies

The tops of these yellow Moon-shaped cookies resemble the surface of the Moon!

Ingredients:
2 sticks butter, softened
2 cups sugar
6 eggs
1 teaspoon vanilla
2 cups flour

Topping:
1/2 cup sugar
1/2 cup chopped nuts

Directions:
Preheat oven to 350°. Cream butter and sugar; then add eggs one at a time. Stir in vanilla and add flour. Mix until well blended. Pour batter into greased jelly-roll pan. For topping, mix together sugar and nuts; then sprinkle the mixture atop the cookie batter. Bake for 10 to 15 minutes. Cool slightly; then cut into Moon shapes. To do this, first cut out a circle of cookie using a round cookie cutter. Set this cookie aside. Then, working from the resulting opening, use the cookie cutter to cut out a variety of Moon shapes.

Jennie Mehigan—Gr. 3, St. Hilary School, Akron, OH

"Sunsations"

Fill your windows with sunshine with this "sunsational" art project. The stained-glass effect will brighten your whole classroom with warm colors.

Materials needed for each child:
10" circle of waxed paper
6" circle and additional scraps of black construction paper
scraps of red, yellow, orange, gold, pink, and purple tissue paper
white glue
scissors

Step 3
waxed paper →

Steps:
1. Fold black circle in half.
2. Cut out the inside to make a circular frame. Cut out rays, eyes, and smile from the construction-paper scraps.
3. Squeeze a thin line of glue in a spiral from the center of the waxed paper outward. Position black circular frame, rays, and features on the waxed paper to make a smiling Sun as shown.
4. Place pieces of tissue paper over the construction-paper Sun, overlapping different colors and covering the waxed paper completely.
5. Dry overnight and peel off the waxed paper.
6. Hang "sunsations" in windows for a stained-glass effect.

Far-Out!

Set the stage for your next space unit with this out-of-sight display! Using colorful paper and various craft materials, create a fictional planet and several of its inhabitants. Attach the resulting cutouts to a bulletin board. From white paper, cut out several large speech bubbles; then label each one with a different fact about the fictional planet along with an Earth-related question. As students learn facts about Earth and its solar system, they can add their own make-believe creatures and planetary facts to the display.

Angie Carpenter—Gr. 2
Hamlow Elementary
Waverly, NE

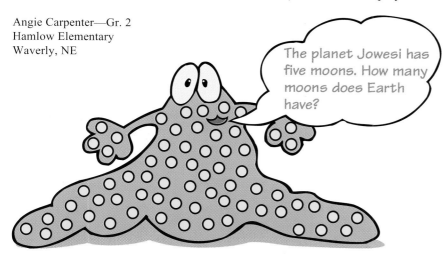

Party On Pluto

This out-of-sight motivational plan encourages stellar student behavior! On a bulletin board covered with black paper, mount cutouts of the Sun and each of the nine planets. Use a pushpin to attach a spaceship cutout to the Sun. Then mount a trail of star cutouts that begins at the Sun, ends on Pluto, and connects all the planets in between. Each time the class demonstrates terrific behavior, move the spaceship forward one star. If the spaceship lands on a planet, reward the class with a special privilege such as five minutes of extra recess. When the spaceship lands on Pluto, treat your youngsters to a well-deserved stellar celebration! Far-out!

Jennifer Ellis—Gr. 3
Tom Green Elementary
Buda, TX

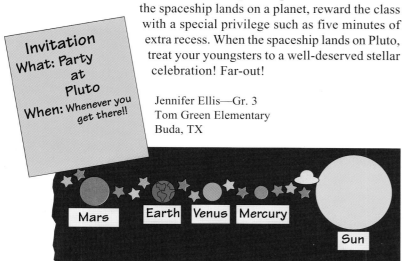

Spaceway Travel Agency

Your students will have a blast creating these planetary posters and they'll be utilizing language skills at the same time. Ask each student to design a poster to advertise a vacation to another planet. (Contact a local travel agency for examples of travel posters to show your class.) Each poster should contain an attention-getting slogan to entice others to travel to the space destination. Students should also include tourist attractions, travel arrangements, and the cost of the trip. Display these zany travel ads on a bulletin board titled "Spaceway Travel Agency."

Laura Horowitz—Gr. 2
Embassy Creek Elementary
Cooper City, FL

Creative Constellations

Send your youngsters into orbit with this star-studded center activity. Place a white crayon, black construction paper, glue, and a supply of small sequins at a center. Also provide several books picturing constellations. After perusing the books, a student creates an original constellation by arranging and gluing sequins on a sheet of black paper. Then, using the white crayon, he writes the name of his constellation on his finished project. Display the completed constellations on a bulletin board entitled "Out-Of-This-World Constellations."

Cynthia Albright
Tyrone, PA

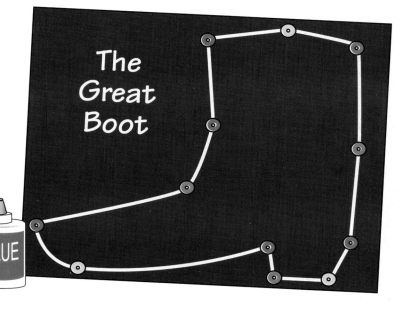

The Great Boot

Planetary Order

To help students remember the order of the planets from the Sun, teach them the following silly sentence: **M**y **V**ery **E**ducated **M**other **J**ust **S**erved **U**s **N**ine **P**izzas. The bold letters stand for the planets Mercury, Venus, Earth, Mars, Jupiter, Saturn, Uranus, Neptune, and Pluto. Invite students to write more silly sentences to remind them of planetary order. Ask each student to write her silly sentence on a construction-paper strip; then mount the reminders where students can easily refer to them.

Laura Horowitz, Plantation, FL

Space Souvenirs

Try this fun finale to your study of the solar system. Have students create souvenirs they might have collected on their journey through our galaxy, such as key rings from Saturn, postcards from Jupiter, or travel posters from Pluto. Provide a variety of art supplies and let your students' imaginations soar out of this world!

Mary Anne Haffner, Waynesboro, PA

Stargazing On Saturn!

If I Were An Astronaut

Out-Of-Sight Stories

These student-made, astronaut-shape booklets are out of this world! To make a booklet, a student colors a white construction-paper copy of the pattern on page 22, adding his own facial features. He cuts out the pattern. Then, using the resulting cutout as a template, he traces and cuts out a supply of shaped writing paper and a construction-paper back cover. He then staples his writing paper between his two covers. Ask each youngster to write his name and date on the first page of his booklet. Explain that the remainder of the booklet is for writing about adventures he thinks he could have as an astronaut. Blast off!

Sandra Maxwell—Gr. 1, W. H. Owen Elementary, Fayetteville, NC

Propel your students' writing enthusiasm to extraordinary heights with this year-round display. Laminate two rocket cutouts; then mount the rockets, the title, and a Moon and several star cutouts as shown. Program each rocket with a type of written work; then invite youngsters to submit corresponding writing samples for the display. Mount students' edited writing atop the star cutouts. Reprogram the rockets each month and keep your students practicing a variety of writing skills.

Amy Turpin—Gr. 2, Murrayville-Woodson Elementary, Murrayville, IL

Showcase your students' special talents at this star-studded display. Have each student lend a hand fingerpainting a large circle cutout. When dry, mount the cutout and attach a paper strip decorated with glitter. Give each student a construction-paper star pattern. Have each student cut out, personalize, and illustrate the pattern. Encourage students to illustrate themselves doing activities that make them feel special. Everyone's a star!

Dianne Knight—Gr. 2, Frank C. Whiteley School, Hoffman Estates, IL

Pattern
Use with "Out-Of-Sight Stories" on page 20.

**If
I Were
An
Astronaut**

Reproducible Activities...

Materials Needed For Each Student

— 1 construction-paper copy of each of the following pages: 25, 27, 29, 31, and 33
— 1 construction-paper copy of the planet fact strips on page 26
— 1 pencil
— scissors
— glue
— crayons
— 1 cotton ball
— 1 small drinking straw
— one 2-centimeter circle cut from a white foam meat tray

Provide the following for students to share:
— sponges for painting
— red, orange, yellow, brown, and white paint
— red Slick® fabric paint (in squeeze bottles)
— green, gold, and blue glitter
— ground pepper

Background For The Teacher

The Sun

The Sun is a star composed of hot gases. It is the center of our solar system. Nine planets orbit around the Sun. They are attracted to the Sun by gravitational force. Proper distance from the Sun provides the right conditions to support life. Earth is the only planet in our solar system with those conditions.

How To Use Pages 25–33 To Make A Solar System Frieze

Discuss each panel of the frieze using the background information and instructions provided on pages 24, 26, 28, 30, and 32. When each child has completed each frieze panel, have him cut out the panels and glue them together end-to-end where indicated. Then ask each child to write the names of the first four planets (the inner planets) on the lines provided on panel 1. Finally have him write the names of the next five planets (the outer planets) on the lines provided on panels 3 and 4. Display the completed projects on a wall in the classroom or hallway.

How To Use Page 25

1. Read aloud the text on the introductory panel and discuss the importance of the Sun in our solar system. Have each child write his name on the line provided.
2. Then have each child use sponges to dab red, yellow, and orange paint on his Sun to make it appear to be a ball of fire and gas.

Finished Sample

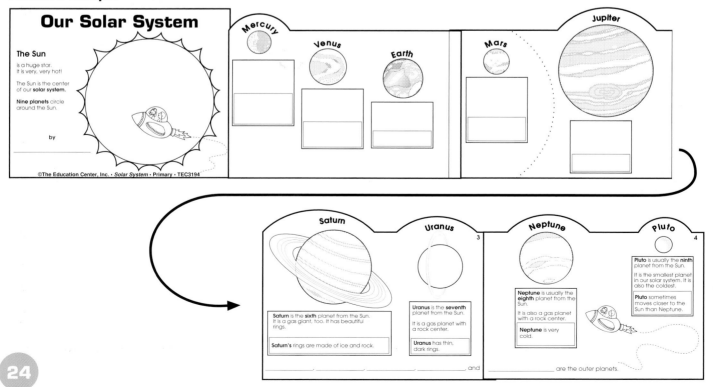

Glue the left edge of panel 1 here.

Our Solar System

The Sun
is a huge star.
It is very, very hot!

The Sun is the center
of our **solar system.**

Nine planets circle
around the Sun.

by

25

How To Use Page 27

1. Read aloud the text about Mercury and discuss its features using the background information on this page.
2. Have each child dip an end of his drinking straw in brown paint and dot the surface of Mercury to make it look like it has craters.
3. Read aloud the text about Venus and discuss its features using the background information on this page.
4. Have students color Venus with a bright color such as yellow. Then have each child add accents with green glitter to make it appear shiny.
5. Read aloud the text about Earth and discuss its features using the background information on this page.
6. Have each child color Earth blue and green; then have him glue small pieces of cotton atop the planet to create clouds.

Background For The Teacher
Planets

Mercury has a desertlike surface of rock that is covered with holes or craters. Because of its craters, Mercury looks much like Earth's Moon. Because Mercury is so close to the Sun, the side facing the Sun can reach 873° F while the side away from the Sun can drop to –360° F.

Venus is wrapped in thick clouds of poisonous gases. The clouds reflect sunlight, so from Earth Venus appears to shine brightly in the night sky. Under the clouds Venus is a hot, dry rocky planet.

Earth is also a planet made of rock, but unlike Mercury and Venus, it has a lot of water. From space, pictures show the land, the water, and the swirls of white clouds that surround Earth. Because of Earth's distance from the Sun—not too close or far—plants, animals, and humans are able to live here.

Planet Fact Strips

Mercury is covered with craters.

Venus looks like a bright star from Earth.

Mars is called the Red Planet.

Earth is our home.

Jupiter is called a gas giant.

Uranus has thin, dark rings.

Saturn's rings are made of ice and rock.

Neptune is very cold.

Pluto sometimes moves closer to the Sun than Neptune.

1

Glue the left edge of panel 2 here.

Earth

Earth is the **third** planet from the Sun.

It is the only planet with a lot of water!

Venus

Venus is the **second** planet from the Sun.

A thick layer of poisonous clouds covers Venus.

Mercury

Mercury is the **first** planet from the Sun.

During the day it is very hot. At night it is very cold.

Write.

_____ , and _____ are _____

How To Use Page 29

1. Read aloud the text about Mars and discuss its features using the background information on this page.
2. Have each child color Mars with a red crayon.
3. Read aloud the text about Jupiter and discuss its features using the background information on this page.
4. Have students color Jupiter with red, yellow, and orange crayons. Then have each child add accents with Slick® fabric paint to show the Great Red Spot.

Background For The Teacher
Planets

Mars is a planet of rocks that was shaped by running water. Its rivers disappeared long ago, leaving it a dry desertlike planet except for its ice caps. Mars's soil is rich in rust (iron oxide), which is why it looks red from space. The sky around Mars even appears pink because the rusty dust is stirred up by strong winds.

Jupiter is the largest planet in our solar system. It is called a gas giant because it has no surface and is composed only of gases. The fast-moving clouds form constant storms on the planet. Red, yellow, orange, tan, and white bands of clouds and gases can be seen from space and continuously change positions. One unchanging feature of Jupiter is its large red spot, which is thought to be an enormous storm.

Glue the left edge of panel 3 here.

2

Jupiter

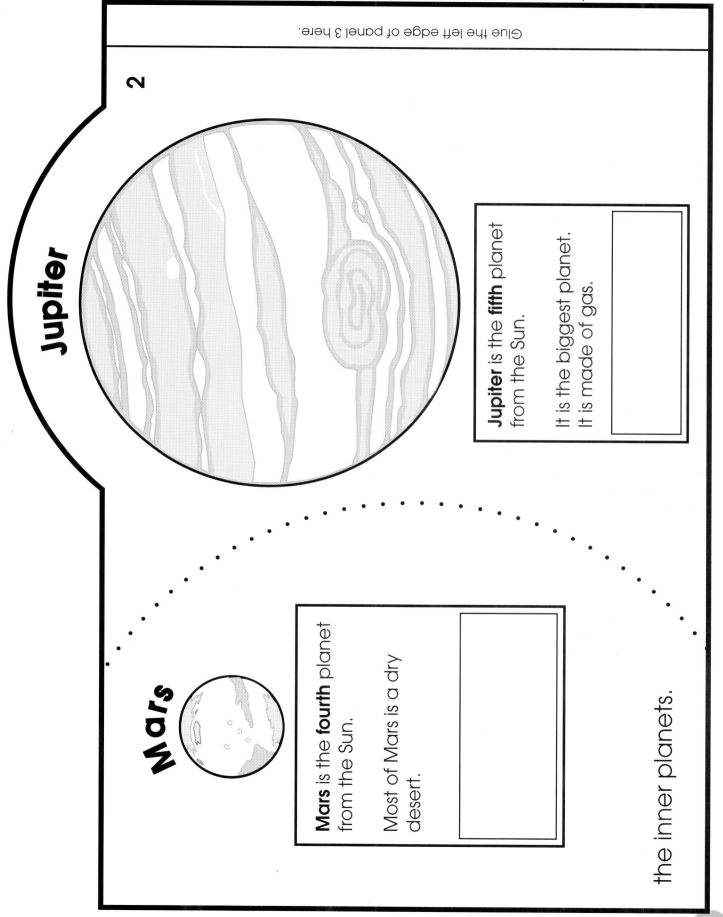

Jupiter is the **fifth** planet from the Sun.

It is the biggest planet. It is made of gas.

Mars

Mars is the **fourth** planet from the Sun.

Most of Mars is a dry desert.

the inner planets.

How To Use Page 31

1. Read aloud the text about Saturn and discuss its features using the background information on this page.
2. Have students use crayons to color yellow and orange bands on Saturn. Then have each child apply glue and gold glitter to the rings circling the planet.
3. Read aloud the text about Uranus and discuss its features using the background information on this page.
4. Have students color Uranus with greenish blue crayons. Then have each child apply glue and a layer of ground black pepper to the rings circling Uranus.

Background For The Teacher

Planets

Saturn, like Jupiter, is composed mostly of gases. It has large rings that look solid from a distance, but are actually made up of thousands of pieces of rock and ice. Saturn's rings give it a beautiful gleaming appearance when scientists see it in the night sky.

Uranus is also a gas giant. The gases that surround this planet give it a greenish blue color. Uranus, like other gas giants, also has rings circling it. The rings of Uranus appear dark and are believed to be made up of dust particles.

Glue the left edge of panel 4 here.

3

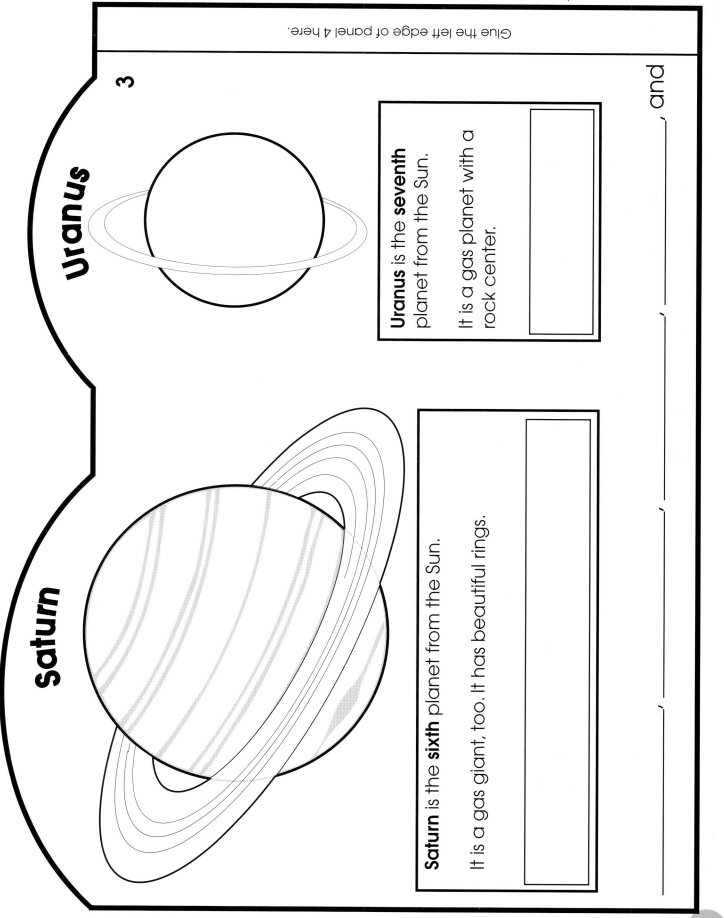

Uranus

Saturn

Uranus is the **seventh** planet from the Sun.

It is a gas planet with a rock center.

Saturn is the **sixth** planet from the Sun.

It is a gas giant, too. It has beautiful rings.

and

Star-Studded Solar System Unit

How To Use Page 33

1. Read aloud the text about Neptune and discuss its features using the background information on this page.
2. Have students use crayons to color Neptune light blue. Then have each child sponge-paint a patchy layer of white paint atop the colored area.
3. Read aloud the text about Pluto and discuss its features using the background information on this page.
4. Have each student roll the edge of his two-centimeter foam circle in glue, then in blue glitter. Then have him glue the disk atop the Pluto drawing.

Background For The Teacher
Planets

Neptune is the last of the gas giants. It is pale blue in color and very far from the Sun. In fact, at times it is the farthest planet from the Sun. It is very hot inside and actually gives off more heat than it receives from the distant Sun. It has not been determined if Neptune has rings like Saturn and Uranus.

Pluto is a tiny planet that is no more than a frozen snowball circling the Sun. It is very different from the gas giants that help make up the outer planets. Pluto circles the Sun in an irregular orbit, sometimes swinging far away from the Sun and at times moving closer. Because of this there are times when Pluto is actually nearer the Sun than Neptune.

4

Pluto

Pluto is usually the **ninth** planet from the Sun.

It is the smallest planet in our solar system. It is also the coldest.

Neptune

Neptune is usually the **eighth** planet from the Sun.

It is also a gas planet with a rock center.

_____ are the outer planets.

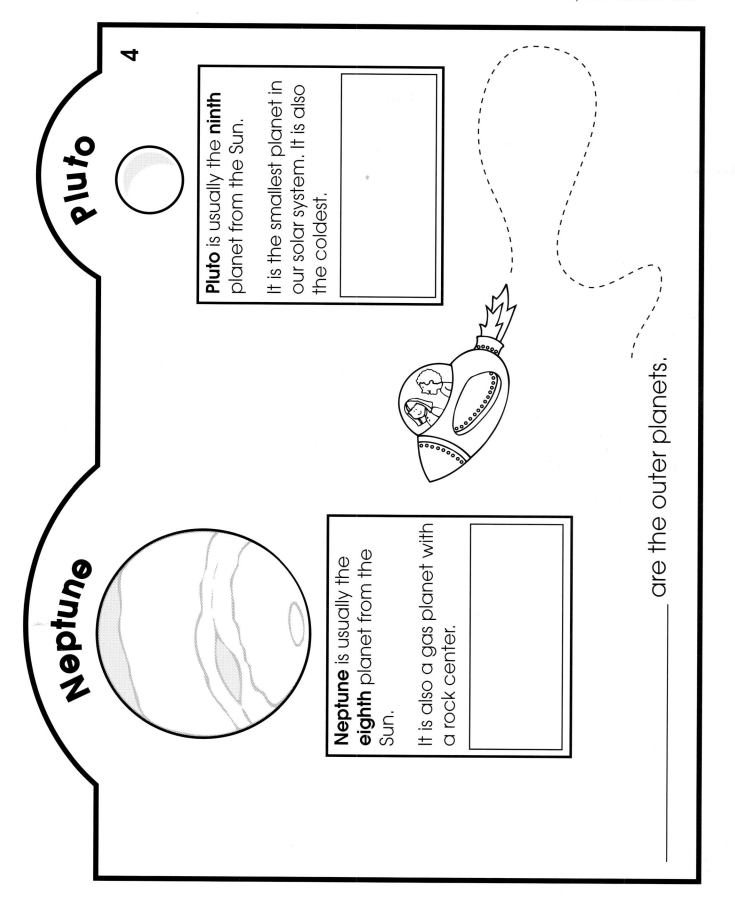

How To Use Page 35

This page is designed to help students research space-related topics like planets, stars, comets, and galaxies. Distribute a copy of page 35 to each student. Instruct each youngster to write the space-related topic he wishes to research in the provided space. Explain that this page is a tool that can be used to organize facts and information. As a class, review the form and discuss any questions or concerns the students have.

When a student's research is complete, he will have the information he needs to write and illustrate a report—or design an informative poster—about his space-related topic.

Answer Key For Page 36

1. We know the most about the planet called E a r t h.
2. This planet is covered with yellow clouds. V e n u s
3. Right next to the Sun is the planet M e r c u r y.
4. This planet looks red to us. M a r s
5. Venus is the brightest p l a n e t.
6. Mars has two potato-shaped m o o n s.
7. We can live on Earth because its air has o x y g e n.
8. Mercury is called the speedy planet because it moves so f a s t.
9. Venus has lots of thunder and lightning, but no r a i n.
10. It is hard to look at Mercury because we look into the S u n.
11. Earth has water for people and animals to d r i n k.
12. Mars has the largest mountain in the solar s y s t e m.
13. Mercury has big holes on it called c r a t e r s.
14. Venus and Earth are almost the same s i z e.
15. Mars has an ice cap at each p o l e.

oxygen
system
Mars
moons
Earth
planet
drink
craters
Venus
fast
size
Sun
Mercury
pole
rain

To solve the riddle, write the letters from the boxes.

What name has been given to the planets **Mercury, Venus, Earth,** and **Mars**?
(Hint: It means Earth-like.)

t e r r e s t r i a l
1. 2. 3. 4. 5. 6. 8. 9. 11. 13. 15.

Answer Key For Page 37

Write a **J** if the phrase tells about Jupiter.
Write an **S** if the phrase tells about Saturn.
Write **JS** if the phrase tells about both.

S   Has seven rings around it.
J   Has a big red spot on it.
J   Is the biggest planet.
J   Is covered with clouds.
J   Is a very hot planet.

J   Makes some of its own heat.
JS Is made up of gases.
S   Is a very cold planet.
S   Is very pretty.
JS Is not made up of rocks.

**Label these planets.
Color them how you think
they might look.**

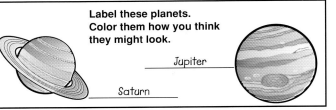

Jupiter

Saturn

Answer Key For Page 38

The planets of Uranus, Neptune, and Pluto are very far away. <u>They are so far away that scientists do not know much about them.</u> They know the most about (Uranus.) It has five moons and at least nine rings. It looks like it is lying on its side. Its rings are very dark and thin. Scientists think that Uranus is covered with clouds. You can only see Neptune and Pluto through a telescope. ~~Two moons have been seen on Neptune.~~ One moon has been seen on Pluto. <u>Pluto is the planet farthest from the Sun.</u>

Circle the names of the nine planets below: Mercury, Venus, Earth, Mars, Jupiter, Saturn, Uranus, Neptune, Pluto.

```
J U P I T E R  V  P L U T O M
U M O R S U N E  U R A N U S
E A R T H L G N E P T U N E
P R I M E R C U R Y R I N G
R S T M O O N S A T U R N P
```

Answer Key For Page 39

1. PLUT**O**
2. S**U**N
3. SAT**U**RN
4. JUPIT**E**R
5. EA**R**TH
    SOLAR SYSTEM
6. MAR**S**
7. NE**P**TUNE
8. UR**A**NUS
9. MER**C**URY
10. V**E**NUS

Brainteaser Answers:

A. solar system
B. outer space

Out-Of-Sight Information

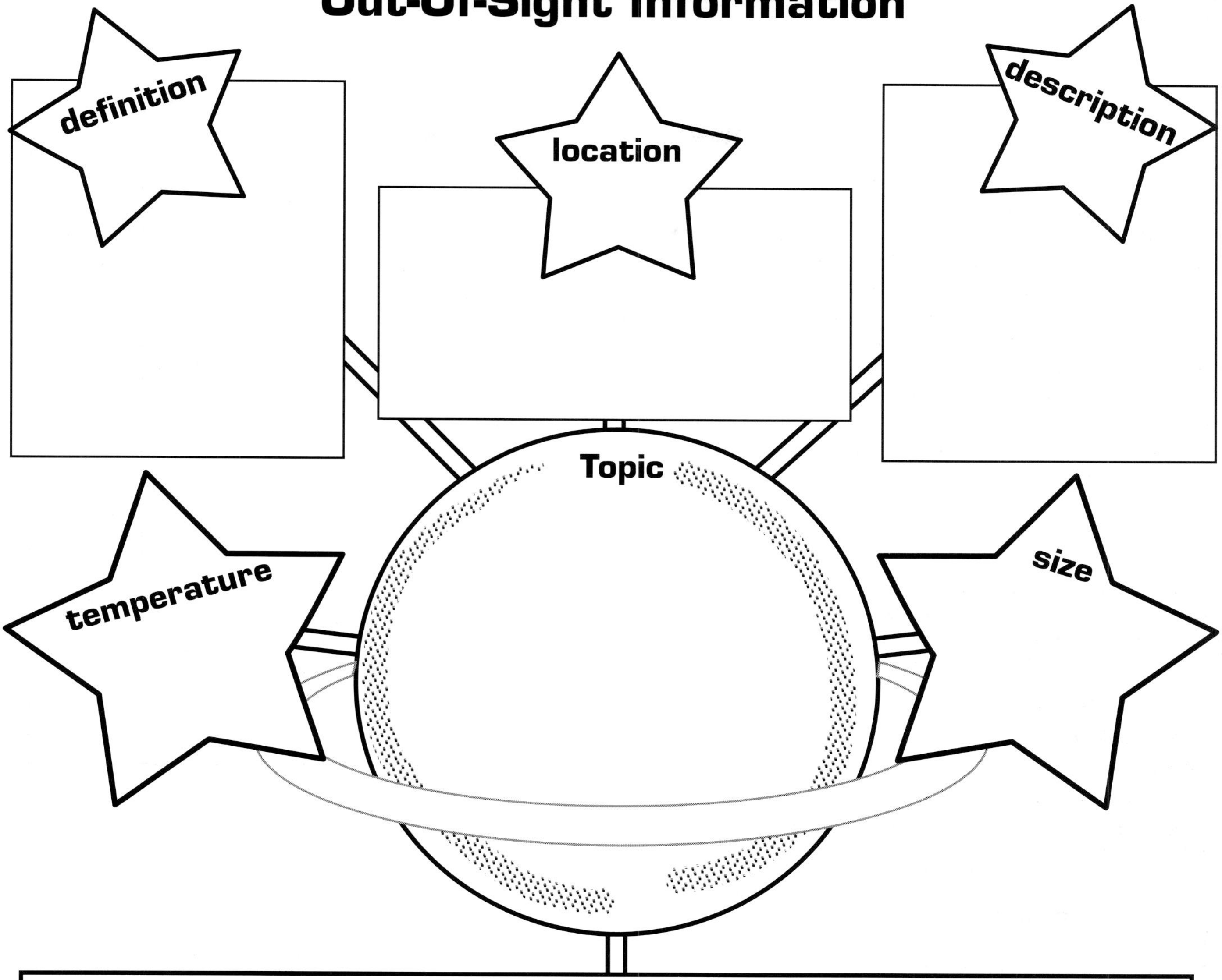

definition

location

description

Topic

temperature

size

Interesting Information

1. _____
2. _____
3. _____
4. _____
5. _____

The Inner Planets

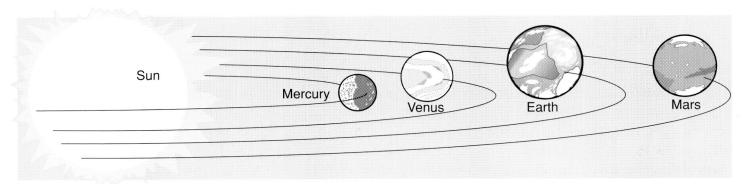

Use the word bank to complete the sentences below.

1. We know the most about the planet called ___ ___ ___ ☐ h .

2. This planet is covered with yellow clouds. V ☐ ___ ___ ___

3. Right next to the Sun is the planet ___ ___ ☐ c ___ ___ ___ .

4. This planet looks red to us. M ___ ☐ ___

5. Venus is the brightest ___ l ___ ___ ☐ ___ .

6. Mars has two potato-shaped ___ o ___ ___ ☐ .

7. We can live on Earth because its air has ___ ___ y ___ ___ ___ .

8. Mercury is called the speedy planet because it moves so f ___ ___ ☐ .

9. Venus has lots of thunder and lightning, but no ☐ ___ i ___ .

10. It is hard to look at Mercury because we look into the ___ ___ n .

11. Earth has water for people and animals to ___ r ☐ ___ ___ .

12. Mars has the largest mountain in the solar ___ ___ s ___ ___ ___ .

13. Mercury has big holes in it called ___ ___ ☐ t ___ ___ ___ .

14. Venus and Earth are almost the same ___ ___ z ___ .

15. Mars has an ice cap at each p ___ ☐ ___ .

Word Bank

oxygen

system

Mars

moons

Earth

planet

drink

craters

Venus

fast

size

Sun

Mercury

pole

rain

To solve the riddle, write the letters from the boxes.

What name has been given to the planets **Mercury, Venus, Earth,** and **Mars?**
(Hint: It means Earth-like.)

___ ___ ___ ___ ___ ___ ___ ___ ___ ___ ___
1.   2.   3.   4.   5.   6.   8.   9.   11.   13.   15.

The Gas Giants

Read the story.

The two biggest planets in our solar system are Jupiter and Saturn. We call them the Gas Giants. This is because they are made up of gases. They are not made up of rocks and metals like Earth.

Jupiter is the biggest planet in our solar system. It is covered with clouds. In the clouds you can see a big red spot. It is shaped like a football. Scientists think this red spot is a giant hurricane. We know that Jupiter has 16 moons. It could have more. Jupiter is a hot planet. It gets some of its heat from the Sun. It also makes heat itself. This makes it different from any other planet in our solar system.

Saturn is the second biggest planet. It is very pretty. It has seven rings around it that glow. Scientists think that Saturn may have 23 moons. Saturn is a very cold planet. It is far away from the Sun. It takes Saturn almost 30 Earth years to make one trip around the Sun.

Write a **J** if the phrase tells about Jupiter.
Write an **S** if the phrase tells about Saturn.
Write **JS** if the phrase tells about both.

_____ Has seven rings around it.   _____ Makes some of its own heat.

_____ Has a big red spot on it.   _____ Is made up of gases.

_____ Is the biggest planet.   _____ Is a very cold planet.

_____ Is covered with clouds.   _____ Is very pretty.

_____ Is a very hot planet.   _____ Is not made up of rocks.

Label these planets.
Color them how you think they might look.

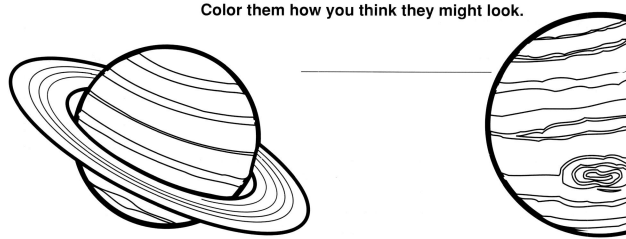

_____

_____

Bonus Box: On another sheet of paper write a fact you learned about Jupiter or Saturn. Cut the words apart. See if a friend can put them back together.

The Mystery Planets

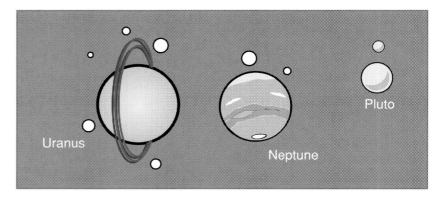

Read this story.

The planets of Uranus, Neptune, and Pluto are very far away. They are so far away that scientists do not know much about them. They know the most about Uranus. It has five moons and at least nine rings. It looks like it is lying on its side. Its rings are very dark and thin. Scientists think that Uranus is covered with clouds. You can only see Neptune and Pluto through a telescope. Two moons have beenseen on Neptune. One moon has been seen on Pluto. Pluto is the planet farthest from the Sun.

Follow these directions.
Use your crayons to mark each answer in the story above.

1. Use your blue crayon. Circle the name of the mystery planet that scientists know the most about.

2. Use your red crayon. Underline the sentence that tells which planet is farthest away from the Sun.

3. Use your brown crayon. Draw a line through the sentence that tells how many moons have been seen on Neptune.

4. Use your yellow crayon. Put an X over the word that names what you must look through to see Neptune and Pluto.

5. Use your green crayon. Underline the sentence that explains why we do not know very much about the mystery planets.

Circle the names of the nine planets below: Mercury, Venus, Earth, Mars, Jupiter, Saturn, Uranus, Neptune, Pluto.

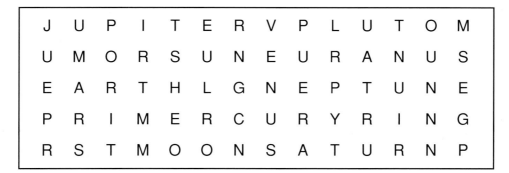

J U P I T E R V P L U T O M

U M O R S U N E U R A N U S

E A R T H L G N E P T U N E

P R I M E R C U R Y R I N G

R S T M O O N S A T U R N P

Name _____

Exploring Space

This puzzle could send you into orbit!

Look at each row of letters. Study the letters near the blank.

Write a letter in the blank to form the name of something found in
  space.

Circle each space word.

The first one has been done for you!

1. Y (P L U T **O**) L W F L V C

2. K M I U S __ N J T H A H

3. G E K S A __ U R N N X D

4. J U P I T __ R V O W Z J

5. P S M E A __ T H Y D T F

    S O L A R ★ S Y S T E M

6. F E M A R __ A X M P R D

7. Q X N N E __ T U N E I P

8. U B Q U R __ N U S O C S

9. E R M E R __ U R Y J R B

10. K M Z A V __ N U S G I L

Brainteaser Box

A. The sun and all the objects that revolve around it have a
   name. What is it? (Hint: Look in the ★ row!)

_____

B. What is everything outside Earth's atmosphere called?
   (Hint: Look at the letters you wrote!)

_____

Bonus Box: On the back of this page, list five more things that are found in space. Make a puzzle like the
one above. Ask a friend to solve it!

Background For The Teacher
The Moon

The Moon—Earth's only natural satellite and its closest neighbor—is an airless ball of rock that is about one quarter the diameter of Earth. It is just over 238,000 miles away—a small distance in space! The Moon circles around Earth once every 29 1/2 days. It has no light of its own, but reflects light from the Sun. Along with the Moon's mountains, hills, valleys, and flatlands there are thousands of bowl-shaped craters that cover its surface. Most of these craters were caused by meteoroids crashing into the Moon billions of years ago. The darker areas on the Moon are *maria,* or seas. These seas were made long ago by lava that flowed from inside the Moon. There is no life on the Moon and there probably never has been. It's really no wonder, since there is no air or water there, and Moon temperatures can range from 250° F during the day to –290° F at night! Because the Moon is lifeless, it has no bright colors. In fact the entire Moon is a dull grayish brown color.

Answer Key For Page 41

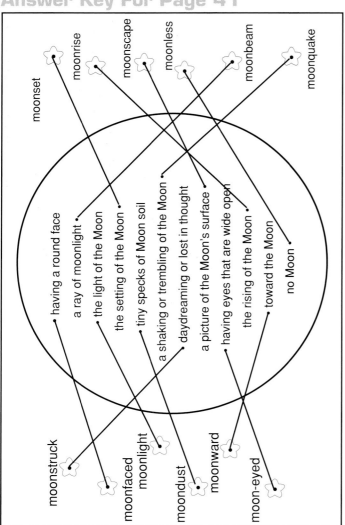

Book Corner
The Moon
Nonfiction

The Sun And Moon • Written by Patrick Moore & Illustrated by Paul Doherty • Copper Beech Books, 1994

The Moon • Written by Seymour Simon; includes photographs • Four Winds Press, 1984

The Moon And You • Written by E. C. Krupp & Illustrated by Robin Rector Krupp • Macmillan Publishing Company, 1993

1000 Facts About Space • Written by Pam Beasant; includes illustrations • Kingfisher Books, 1992

Moon Lore

Moon Magic: Stories From Asia • Retold by Katherine Davison & Illustrated by Thomas A. Rosborough • Carolrhoda Books, Inc.; 1994

The Woman In The Moon: A Story From Hawaii • Retold by Jama Kim Rattigan & Illustrated by Carla Golembe • Little, Brown And Company; 1996

Anansi The Spider: A Tale From The Ashanti • Retold & Illustrated by Gerald McDermott • Henry Holt And Company, 1987

The Moon Lady • Retold by Amy Tan & Illustrated by Gretchen Schields • Aladdin Paperbacks, 1995

Moon Fiction

Armadillo Ray • Written by John Beifuss & Illustrated by Peggy Turley • Chronicle Books, 1995

Possum's Harvest Moon • Written & Illustrated by Anne Hunter • Houghton Mifflin Company, 1996

The Squirrel And The Moon • Written & Illustrated by Eleonore Schmid • North-South Books, Inc.; 1996

Name _____

Lunar Lingo

There are many Moon-related words in our language.
Match each Moon-related word to its definition.
Use a ruler to connect the black dots.

moonset •

moonrise •

moonscape •

moonless •

moonbeam •

moonquake •

• having a round face

a ray of moonlight •

• the light of the Moon

the setting of the Moon •

• tiny specks of Moon soil

a shaking or trembling of the Moon •

• daydreaming or lost in thought

a picture of the Moon's surface •

• having eyes that are wide open

the rising of the Moon •

• toward the Moon

no Moon •

moonstruck •

moonfaced •

• moonlight

moondust •

• moonward

moon-eyed •

Bonus Box: Now that you are a pro at lunar lingo, make up a definition for each of these
made-up moon words! Write each word and its meaning on the back of this paper.
moondance   moonmilk   moonhat

41

How To Use Page 43

1. Share with students some information about Moon exploration (see "Background For The Teacher: Moon Exploration"). If desired, read aloud a related picture book—perhaps one of the suggested titles in "Book Corner: Moon Exploration."
2. Introduce the activity by reading aloud the first two sentences on the page. Challenge students to recall the special message that was engraved on the plaque. Discuss the message (located in the background information on this page).
3. Have each student complete the activity by following the provided directions.
4. Set aside time for students to share their completed work with their classmates.

Book Corner
Moon Exploration

Grandpa Takes Me To The Moon • Written by Timothy R. Gaffney & Illustrated by Barry Root • Tambourine Books, 1996

The Sea Of Tranquillity • Written by Mark Haddon & Illustrated by Christian Birmingham • Harcourt Brace & Company, 1996

Background For The Teacher
Moon Exploration

The space age, which began in 1957, opened a new chapter in the study of the Moon. The Soviet Union and the United States launched numerous unmanned spacecraft that either landed on the Moon or passed close enough to send back useful information. On July 20, 1969, United States astronauts Neil Armstrong and Edwin "Buzz" Aldrin landed the Apollo 11 lunar module *Eagle* on the Moon, left the module, and explored the lunar surface firsthand. These first human Moon visitors left behind a plaque that read "Here men from the planet Earth first set foot upon the Moon. July 1969 A.D. We came in peace for all mankind." Between December 1968 and December 1972, men from Earth made nine voyages to the Moon as part of America's Apollo program. The voyages included six lunar landings with a total of 12 men walking on the Moon's surface. These astronauts explored and photographed the lunar landscape, gathered samples of Moon rocks and soil, and set up various scientific experiments. The explorations provided scientists with enough material for years of Moon study. All explorers returned safely. Since 1972, there have been no Moon visitors. Today the Moon is a symbol of peaceful exploration of space. A space exploration treaty signed in 1967 by more than 90 nations declares that neither the Moon nor any other natural body in outer space may be claimed by any country or be used for military purposes.

Moon Landing!

The first men who landed on the Moon left an American flag.
They also left a plaque that was engraved with a special message.

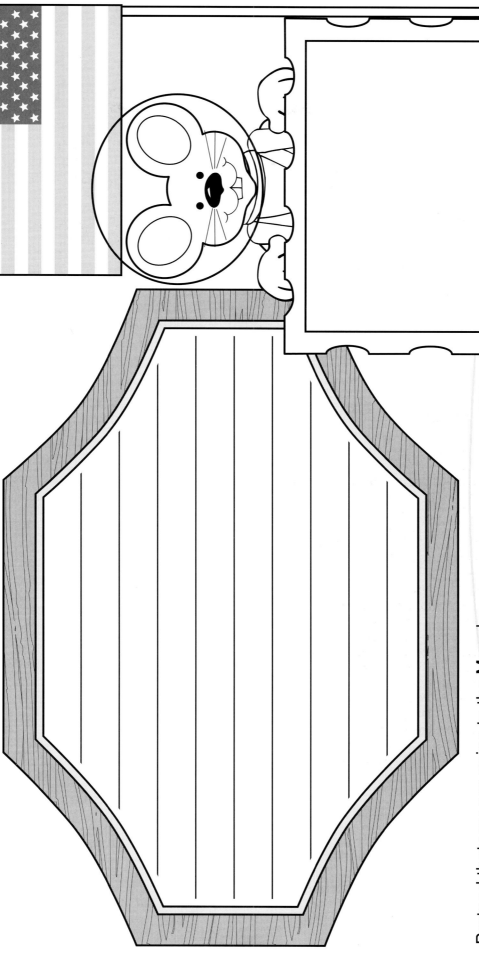

Pretend that you are going to the Moon!
On the plaque above, write a message for future Moon visitors to read.
Then draw and color a snapshot of yourself landing on the Moon.
In the snapshot show what else you will take to the Moon.

©The Education Center, Inc. • *Solar System* • Primary • TEC3194

43

Marvelous Moon Unit

Materials Needed For Each Student

— white construction-paper copy of page 45
— pencil
— yellow and black crayons (or markers)
— scissors
— glue

How To Use Page 45

1. To explain and illustrate the phases of the Moon, draw a horizontal row of nine circles on the chalkboard. Then, using the information in "Background For The Teacher: Phases Of The Moon," explain, illustrate, and label the phases as shown below.
2. Distribute the activity and have each student personalize the cover (titled "Moon Phases") and color the Moon shape yellow. Then have each child color each Moon phase by using her yellow crayon to show the part of the Moon that is reflecting sunlight and her black crayon to show the part of the Moon that is not.
3. Then have each student assemble her booklet.

Booklet Assembly Directions For The Student

1. Cut out each pattern piece along the bold lines. Do not cut on the thin lines.
2. To create one long pattern piece, lay the cutouts end-to-end so that the Moon's phases are in the correct order.
3. Glue the cutouts together where shown to create one long strip.
4. Using the thin lines as guides, accordion-fold the pages. (Demonstrate this step and provide assistance as needed.)

Background For The Teacher

Phases Of The Moon

As the Moon moves around Earth, it keeps the same side facing Earth. On Earth we see a varying amount of this side, depending on how much of the side is being lit by the Sun. These apparent changes in the Moon's shape are called the *phases of the Moon*. The Moon orbits Earth once every 29 1/2 days. During this *lunar month,* the Moon changes from a *new moon* (no reflection of sunlight) into a *full moon* (the entire side of the Moon is lit by the Sun), then back to a new moon. After a new moon, the Moon *waxes,* or grows, into the *crescent phase* (less than half of the side is lit), to the *first quarter phase* (half of the side is lit), to the *gibbous phase* (more than half of the side is lit). The next Moon phase is the *full moon* which means the entire side of the Moon is lit. A full moon occurs about 14 or 15 days into a lunar month. Next the Moon appears to *wane,* or shrink. During this time the Moon phases appear in reverse order—gibbous, last quarter, and crescent phase—until the Moon completely disappears, which indicates another new moon. The Moon phases' process then begins again.

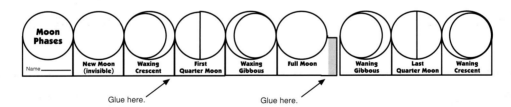

Glue here.   Glue here.

Illustration Of Moon Phases

| New Moon | Waxing Crescent | First Quarter Moon | Waxing Gibbous | Full Moon | Waning Gibbous | Last Quarter Moon | Waning Crescent | New Moon |

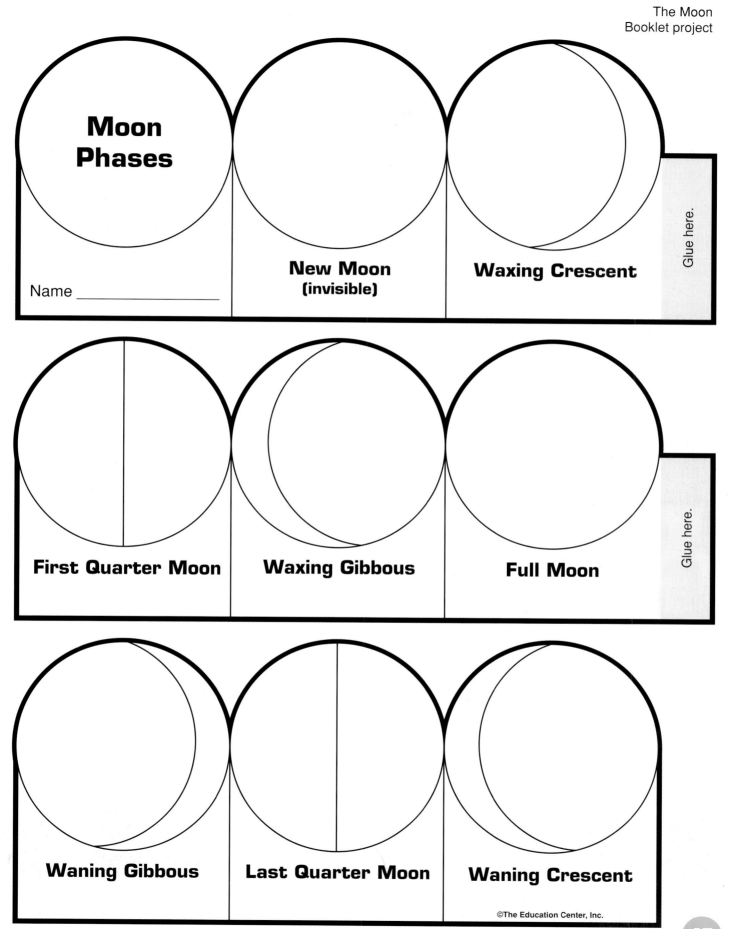

Moon Phases

Name _____

New Moon (invisible)

Waxing Crescent

Glue here.

First Quarter Moon

Waxing Gibbous

Full Moon

Glue here.

Waning Gibbous

Last Quarter Moon

Waning Crescent

©The Education Center, Inc.

45

"Sun-sational" Sun Unit

How To Use Page 47

Read aloud to students the text on the booklet pages. Give students time to complete the drawings on the pages. Then provide assistance by punching holes in the pages and cutting yarn to attach the booklet pages together.

Materials Needed

—white construction-paper copies of page 47
—scissors
—hole punch
—yarn

Directions For The Student

1. Draw the picture indicated on each page.
2. Cut out the booklet pages.
3. Have your teacher punch holes at the ●'s.
4. String the pages together with yarn and tie a bow.
5. Take your "My Sun Book" home and share it with your family.

Answer Key For Page 48

1. No
2. We are closer to the Sun.
3. It bubbles like boiling soup.
4. The Sun is so bright that it can hurt our eyes.
5. The Sun is the shape of a ball.
6. The Sun

Background For The Teacher

The Sun

It is the Sun's gravity that keeps Earth in its orbit around the Sun. Without the Sun, Earth would freeze and life, as we know it, would cease to exist. Our seasons occur because of the tilt of Earth as it travels around the Sun. Night and day occur because of Earth's rotation upon its axis.

Shadows are also caused by the Sun. Shadows will always occur on the side of the object that is opposite the Sun. The size of the shadow is affected by the Sun's position in the sky. The higher in the sky the Sun is, the shorter the shadow will be. Therefore, at noon, when the Sun is highest in the sky, a shadow is short. In the morning or late afternoon, when the Sun is lower in the sky, shadows appear longer.

The Sun is actually a medium-sized star. The Sun looks bigger and gives us more heat and light than the other stars because it is closer to us. Although it is the closest star, the Sun is still 93 million miles away! The Sun is over 100 times wider than Earth. It takes only eight minutes and 20 seconds for the Sun's heat and light to travel the distance to Earth. However, only about two-billionths of the Sun's light and heat reach Earth. The rest is lost in space. Remind students never to look directly at the Sun since it will harm their eyes.

Extension Activities

— The Sun is so large that it would take 100 Earths lined up side by side to stretch across its diameter. Help students visualize the size of the Sun in comparison to Earth using pennies. Tell your students to imagine one penny as the size of Earth. On the playground, have students line up 100 pennies side by side in a straight line. Then measure out a piece of string the length of 50 pennies in the line. Have one student stand at the center of the line (penny #50) and hold one end of the string. The teacher takes the other end of the string and, with a piece of chalk, traces a circle on the playground around the line of pennies. This circle shows the relative size of the Sun to Earth.

— On a bright day, allow students to experiment outside with shadows. Trace one child's shadow in the morning, again at noon, and once more before leaving for the day. Make sure the child always stands in the same place, facing in the same direction each time. Shadows of different lengths, spreading out in different directions, should result.